THE BODY
IS NO
MACHINE

New Issues Poetry & Prose

Managing Editor   Marianne Swierenga

Copy Editor   Elizabeth Marzoni

Assistant to the Editor Kimberly Kolbe

New Issues Poetry & Prose
The College of Arts and Sciences
Western Michigan University
Kalamazoo, MI 49008

First Edition, 2007.

ISBN-10   1-930974-69-8 (paperbound)
ISBN-13   978-1-930974-69-2 (paperbound)

Library of Congress Cataloging-in-Publication Data:
Perrine, Jennifer
The Body Is No Machine/Jennifer Perrine
Library of Congress Control Number: 2006937311

Art Director   Tricia Hennessy
Designer   Lauren French
Production Manager   Paul Sizer
                      The Design Center, School of Art
                      College of Fine Arts
                      Western Michigan University

To Jamie,
Fellow madwoman!
Thanks for respecting & keeping
alive the lexicon!

THE BODY
IS NO
MACHINE

JENNIFER PERRINE

Jennifer Perrine
Pittsburgh
11-4-09

New Issues

 WESTERN MICHIGAN UNIVERSITY

Contents

How Clay Becomes Flesh

The Night in Her Mouth

Time and Song Enough

Fiancée of Death

Clicks and Whirrs

Shift of Dirt

Acknowledgements:

Grateful acknowledgement is made to the editors of the following journals, in which these poems first appeared, some in earlier versions or under different titles:

Antietam Review: "Broken Sonnet"

Apalachee Review: "Out on My Birthday, October 8, 1998"

Bellingham Review: "Because You're No Magician," "My Mother Learns the Language of Pregnancy"

Connecticut River Review: "Genesis: On the Seventh Day"

The Cream City Review: "Portrait of D., After the First Operation," "Brood X," "Ballad for My Sweetheart the Drunk," "In Praise of the Myoclonic Jerk"

Ellipsis: "Tullio's *Adam*"

Gertrude: "Photograph of My Grandparents on the Farm, August 1945"

Green Mountains Review: "The Amputation of My Brother's Finger," "To the Ghost in My Front Yard"

Harpur Palate: "When the Palm Reader Sees That You Have Two Life Lines, He Says You Must Choose One"

Inkwell: "The Body Is No Machine," "Dysmorphia," "Pica"

The Ledge: "The Weight," "To Mirah: In Utero: On Being Named"

Nimrod: "*Ex Ovo Omnia*"

Paterson Literary Review: "Elegy for Mrs. Donnell"

The Peralta Press: "Mission Hill Lament"

Poems & Plays: "Coveting, with Pronunciation Guide"

Quarterly West: "For D., After Three Months on Testosterone," "Gender Question #2: Butch, Femme, Androgynous, or All Over the Map?," "I'm in Love with a Tooth Grinder," "In Response to Your Attempts at Seduction," "The Second Song of Miriam"

Red Wheelbarrow: "Mother as Rope"

Redivider: "Ballad for a Goth Chick," "Ménage à Trois with Two Women and an Imaginary Man"

RHINO: "The Resurrectionist's Wife," "Sadie Imagines God"

River Styx: "To My Cannibalized Twin"

Southern Poetry Review: "Buzz"

The Sow's Ear Poetry Review: "Broken Sonnet," "In Honor of Your Birthday, I've Been Mauled By a Dog"

Willow Springs: "My First Stripper," "When You Ask Whether I Ever Played with Dolls"

I am also grateful to Florida State University for the fellowships that enabled me to complete this collection. Sincere thanks to my many mentors and colleagues at Florida State University, Bucknell University, and Susquehanna University—you have sustained me with your support and encouragement. Finally, love and gratitude to the poets whom I have been blessed to call friends—Stacey Waite, Matt Perakovich, Susanna Childress, Sara Pennington, and Dominika Wrozynski—and to my family, especially Chris Purcell, for patience approaching sainthood.

How Clay Becomes Flesh

My Mother Learns the Language of Pregnancy

Not in freshman science, where reproduction was nothing
less than an arabesque of cells duplicating—alike,
alike—one species' biotic potential slopping

its Bronx cheer at death. The orphanage kept its classroom
communications pared to mitosis, the flatworm's
totipotency, its severed half regenerating

on the ocean floor—so maybe my mother, learning
English under the gaze of nuns, didn't understand
St. Augustine's claim—*we are born between feces*

and urine—or maybe she could only imagine
one body growing inside another the way the disk
of Christ swaddled in wine plumped with her saliva.

Safe to say, at fifteen, with a fetus already
holding sway in her womb, my mother couldn't quite make
sense of the doctor or his drawings: the one he called

fertilization—queen in her round hive swarming
with a spermatozoal onrush—looked like nothing
so much as the workings of water bugs on a pond,

or the legless lizards that slunk across the floor
of her kitchen back in Peru. If she knew how,
she would have said her whole body felt *gingival*, tender

as the space left by a tooth, or *incandescent*, a rash
of izles flicking the dark, but she had only the scent
of the words, the slack weight of them like fat in her throat,

the same throat that would expand to make room for *chorion*,
diameter, exile, that years later would shake
like a husk while she fumbled with the reins of her tongue,

loosing its testimony, trying to explain the child
left on the pink stone steps, the one waiting patiently
as graffiti in the fingers of a vandal.

Pica

This is how clay becomes flesh: dirt and grit
clumping with saliva, bits of sand wedged

between gum and tooth. In my mother's mouth:
her palate alive with humus: a crush

of chalk threading down her throat: and somewhere
deep within her gut: a Galatea,

milk white, translucent: a creature she'll bring
together from pulverized stone. She's sure

all desire begins with me: my unborn,
indiscriminate taste, my unwieldy

appetite for handfuls of ash and soil:
and when I'm born, though she gives me a name

plain and utile as toothpaste, she insists
on calling me Magpie: and how she's right:

when I'm first caught filling my cavernous
maw with paint chips, plaster, coffee grounds pulled

from the trash, my father reassures her:
this is the work of all infants: to hold

the world inside them, piece by piece: to turn
each sliver about on the tongue: a shape

in a tangram: a code the child's mouth cracks.
But when my mother finds me, years later:

a toddler, plucking flies from the window:
the curse slithers out of her: *freak*: as though

she's never enjoyed this comfort: as though
she doesn't remember reaching for more.

In Honor of Your Birthday, I've Been Mauled By a Dog

And on the gurney—my leg being swabbed
by a doctor whose hands, even through latex,
are cold—I'm guessing what you're doing tonight:
creolizing in your kitchen, socked feet
propped on formica, a cigarette bogarted
between your lips. You're working through logic
puzzles with erasable pen, tapping
its plastic along your teeth while you think
of crosses and dots and maybe your children,
how we felt in you, like the lumps of fluid
swelling the surface of my calf, bloated
bellies stretching teeth marks. When I'm discharged,
I won't call, though I'll think about it, hobbling
home to the kiss of my crutch against concrete.

Mother as Rope

Strange how you always remember her
angry, her mouth cinched tight as a knot,
then letting that coarseness spill, her lips
the loop through which heat passed,
her jaw straining against its hitches,
then slack, limp, when she'd run
out of breath.
        This is the way her lips
looked that day, nooselike, while you twisted
tissues in your hands. All that time,
dusky filaments entwining her lungs,
then the braid of her spine, which coiled
itself with kinks no massage would undo,
and when she left you, finally, your hands
were on her back, still kneading,
rubbed raw with loss.
        Just as her memory
rotted through in the end, wound taut
around a dead, fibrous center, you say
your memory of her has begun to fray
into threads you pull, like white hairs
from her shoulders.

Ex Ovo Omnia

A newborn dubbed "The Monster of Ravenna" was
starved to death by order of Pope Julius II in 1512.

And what of the mother of the monster,
    the Pandora's box of her womb? What crack

in the world did she peer through to impress
    this upon her child: eagle's foot and horned

head, serpents dripping from its waist, bat wings
    folded over a superfluous eye?

What can we say for the mother except
    from the egg, all—newt and rodent, human

and worm? What could she know of genetics:
    cistrons that pump out seven hearts, twin mouths,

or a form more common, more humble? What
    could she do but watch while her infant starved?

What could she do but what we all do—hold
    our faults close, their names like stones on our tongues?

To My Cannibalized Twin

Whatever you were or might have been: orb,
lump, dim glow beside me, some human shard
of glitter, pearled sand in our mother's paunch:
I tell you now you were lucky, uncaged

by my misfit hunger. You can regard
it a kindness: my desire to absorb
has always been here, waiting to get drunk
on the next heart, imbibe a look through veiled

eyes, suck the tongue of somebody's pigtailed
beloved. Tell me, stranger, lonely monk
hovering somewhere in my cells, engaged

in whatever thankless task my young greed
assigned you: if you were here, could you staunch
this wanting, make me cough up its sharp seed?

Couvade Aubade

Again, I wake to the song
    of his retching, to the bergamot

and vinegar scent of bile.
    He's doubled up on the bathroom tile,

hands cupping his tumescent
    belly, the slow rub of his fingers

slipping the skin back and forth
    like the flesh of an overripe peach,

caressing it like a breast,
    as if it would leak colostrum thick

with extravagance, spill it
    onto the floor. When I bend to kiss

him, his mouth hatches a breath
    luscious as envy, green with longing.

The Night in Her Mouth

Coveting, with Pronunciation Guide

And what if I said your breasts rise
like an umlaut over the *o* of your stomach?
That I have imagined two hipbones, grave
and acute, inflecting legs long as vowels,
ohs and *oohs*, the tendons at the backs
of your knees taut as macrons? Who else
will tell you how your top lip lurks
over your teeth like a tilde, the small list
of your smirk to the left?
                      Let me whisper you
seduction like a cedilla, soft and complex,
an arcing voice full of hooks and barbs.
Let me rest the circumflex of my hands, tented,
tentative, against your waist. Let my body
be a breve, the cup into which you drop
your breath. Let desire be clumsy
as a schwa, upside-down, almost soundless.

I'm in Love with a Tooth Grinder

How she crushes the fine bones of her dreams
like so much grist, turns the night
in her mouth. I love the sound of her slow cud

movement, her sympathy for the counted sheep,
how she'll ruminate for hours and come up
with nothing but her own circular thrum,

mantra of the clenching jaw, meditation
on the erosion of the body.
I think she wants to tell me what burdens

she polishes behind her lips: the pestle
rasping at its mortar, the whistle
of knife against wheel,

adrenaline weeping of brakes,
slow sliding halt of the world.
We learn to sleep

with that hum of friction,
with the moon rubbing up
against our shadows, begging to touch us,

with the strange lullaby of our skin
against the sheets, the soft hymn of our legs
scratching together in the dark.

To My Love: Before Surgery: Asleep in Bed

On the upended crate
    that we've christened *end table*: this heap

of trappings you carry
    by day: an accumulated *you*

puddled beside the bed:
    the belt curled upon itself, earrings

stuck through one of its holes,
    your glasses squinting into the dark.

Once, this space would have spent
    the night empty: so eager for sleep

or each other we came
    to bed clothing and all: no washing

the day from our faces,
    no careful dismantling of the selves

in which we'd suited up.
    Now, still awake long after you've thrown

yourself wholeheartedly
    into the tumult of dreams, I run

my hands over each piece
    cast off, as if I could find the parts

not yet acquired: the wig
    you'll don when worry has thinned you out,

the row of teeth shining
    moonlight from their beatific smile.

To My Love: After Surgery: Asleep in Public

In sleep, all the hump and deft design
    of your body dissolves

into its hard burden of angles:
    a jag of hair poked out

from your skull, the crook of an elbow
    against your chest, and each

canthus flattened into a thin line
    that flits beneath the pulse

and churn of your dreaming eyes: and though
    this bent version of you

wants to summon your future ghost: bag
    of spikes and spindles left

after cachexia planes the sweet
    bulk and heft of you—no:

all this folding says instead *alive*,
    says *animal*: burrow

of your chin into my shoulder, sharp
    grunt and scratch as you shift

in your seat: here you are plunged so far
    back through life, back until

you know nothing but the float and sway
    of the world hustling you

along, the rush of your deserter
    lungs, the slug of your heart.

24

Because You Have No Sense of Smell

I will not speak of perfumes: let me say
    your scent is the blue tinge rimming skim milk,

the rustle of barely opaque pages
    in a Bible. You said my skin tasted

only of salt, but I say it's the whirr
    and buzz of a moth trapped between window

and screen. In our bed, saliva lingered
    on my lips, round as a strawberry seed

discovered in some nook of my mouth; and
    on summer nights, our sweat fine as vapor,

aromatic as a phosphorescent
    smudge against the dark. After, every breath

I drew came out of me scintillated,
    fragrant as dust swimming in sheets of light.

Tullio's *Adam*

Tullio Lombardo's Renaissance sculpture, Adam, *crashed
to the ground in the Metropolitan Museum on October 6, 2002,
when the base of its pedestal apparently buckled.*

This time, when Adam fell,
it wasn't for a taste
of free will, but a kiss

of open-mouthed marble.
His lips caressed the floor
with their parted heart, milk

stone splintering, spilling
from his imagined tongue.
Under chance's embrace,

his whole body shivered
into shards. The thick slabs
of his legs, wrapped around

museum air, settled
in a shower of dust.
This time, Temptation dressed

simply, wearing only
the cold promise of rest,
her slice of crowbar smile.

My First Stripper

was named Robin, and yes, her breasts *were* red
as she winnowed the weeds from her garden.

She was the kind of woman my mother
always warned me about—*don't you go near*

that apartment downstairs—but how could I
have resisted the daggers, those bright blades

that slipped from the hem of her shorts, their ink
climbing into the sun, trying to touch

the grass where she knelt? As I remember,
only her face escaped the stained-glass trail

of tattoos: the dueling hummingbirds
with intercrossed proboscises

flanking the straight stretch of her spine, a pair
of dice perched on her sternum, the haloed

Virgin competing with *Lucky Seven*
for the privacy where her neck was cloaked

by hair. Still too young to imagine her
swirling in soft purple light, ballasted

by a metal pole, when my mother hissed
stripper, I could only envision this:

Robin, running her hands along her legs,
as if to remove stockings, and under

her fingers, a unicorn skitters down
to the ground, poker chips pool around her

ankles, birds lift into the air, colors
flung like parachutists, humming with light.

In Response to Your Attempts at Seduction

I'll be like the dolmen, slab
and stone, unmoved for centuries,

or otherwise prehistoric, grunting,
scuttling back to my cave.

I'll be the albedo of the lake,
tessellate whatever slick light

you shine, but all surface,
no dabbling, no quick fingers

threading through water.
I won't touch you,

but if I do, I'll be
only the virga, vapor

whispering her skirts
above earth's upturned face,

or dendritic, fondling
synapses, reaching you only

by impulse. I won't be
italic, leaning into you

with weighted meaning,
or helix, weaving

my legs around yours.
I'll be somnambulant,

walking alone, waking up
in the dark hall of your throat,

hollow as the lumen
of a needle, of a vein.

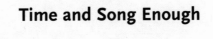

Time and Song Enough

Brood X

Listen: the droning buzz its own horology,
the slow aggression of clocks. Some seventeen-year
itch draws them out of the dirt, cicadas suckled

by roots, ambrosial water eked out in the dark.
You said they sang like Satan's parakeets, their thrum
so thick you wished your ears more like your mouth, so full

of voluntary muscle. That sound says, *savor*,
one vibration rolls over the next, like your tongue
fondling a knot of tart berries or your own name,

how you could say it, *Emily*, like an adverb
modifying your whole unkempt world. And isn't
this how change always begins, time and song enough

to slough off the cells of who you once were, to live
by slow feed, growing into your body, not quite
holometabolic, nothing so dramatic

as a chrysalis cast off like a linen dress,
no leaping from a ledge into new life, surprised
at your own flannelled weightlessness—but nonetheless

a resurrection of that girl you were, walking
alone at night, no one yet behind you, the punch
of your hips against the dark, as though they had borne

holsters: your boldness, one flourish for the passing
cars, another for this remembered year swimming
around you like a gyroscope: torque, axis, spin.

For D., After Three Months on Testosterone

When you sent me that clip
of your voice, I cried. Stupid, I admit
to mourn half an octave,

to elegize vibration, how one lip
departed, full, scarlet,
and came back to the other, more furtive,

inscrutable, that strip
of dark down growing thick as a secret.
You said it's adaptive,

like moths that, between generations, slip
into a new palette,
survival mostly a means to outlive

your old skin, to unzip
yourself and trade that ill-fitting outfit
for one more transitive.

Portrait of D., After the First Operation

After surgery, your breasts: two keyholes
where your nipples once were. You showed
me the tattoo you'd stitched from one
flat slope to the other, the serpent winding
behind your neck like another kind of boa,
feathers of ink licking your chest. I can't
imagine holding you now without wanting
to undo those lines like the slinky strings
of a bikini: to tug your skin until something
falls free between us. When you say you feel
more vulnerable as a man, I think, it's true,
you've brought your scars outside: you,
wincing in the light, the air new, thick
as a hand under your unbuttoned shirt.

Ménage à Trois with Two Women and an Imaginary Man

> "A State College woman was convicted Friday of pretending to be
> a Texas cattleman seeking love over a CB radio in order to scam
> lonely women out of more than $100,000 [. . .] During the trial,
> Morrow said she pretended to be a man because she was lonely."
> —*The Daily Item*

There's only one kind of woman: patience
worn to a fine sheen, to a flimsy strap,
to the faint *thick thick* of sandals kissing
a dirt road. She knows how to fill the gap

between the static and the drawl curling
from the speakers in her basement, between
the cowboy she carves into the darkness
and the woman who comes now to the screen

door, regular as church, with promises
to send the money on to Texas. She's
never been fooled: fantasy an earring
that glints through her veil of hair, the chemise

she dons when company calls, how she'll sing
all day, remembering his laugh and moan
in another woman's mouth: that caress
she'll steal back to later when she's alone.

Gender Question #2: Butch, Femme, Androgynous, or All Over the Map?

Marking the small check in the small box,
I think: there is no appropriate answer here,
except perhaps *Artichoke*, impenetrable, thick-petaled
flower, sharp edge and ragged root. Inside,
velvet opal translucent tongues, and inside,
further still, the choke, silky threads who want
to hold in the heart, to raise a spired fortress
for the tender green. This, though, is not an option,

so I choose, *All over the map*, all over Barbados,
Siam, Constantinople, all over Ireland and Israel,
all over the sierra of my stomach, down the straits
of my legs, to the archipelago of toes.
Somewhere on the circuit, I stop

to visit whatever terrain bears the name *Femme*,
some scenic dream atop a mountain or nestled
deep within a delta. I watch tourists teem
around the attractions. I snap some shots, too,
so I'll remember what Femme looks like
once I leave. Perhaps, from there, I'll bike

to *Butch*, a city that sparkles like hubcaps
spun from a swift machine. Some say that there
the stars are drilled through sheets of obsidian,
pressed like grommets into hides of darkest leather.
If the iron gates to town are barred, I'll fly

first-class to *Androgynous*, where blades of grass glow
silver, the shade of Joan of Arc's sword,
and the sky at sunset runs red as the rouge
on Bowie's cheeks. The land shifts,
rolls and recedes like the tide, carries me out

39

and out, to my home, my artichoke home,
my platypus home, my webbed feet
and beak and fur. I trace again my small mark
in my small box, my small window
from which I watch landscapes reach
like frail fingers into space,
into the places we have not named.

Buzz

My first time was in some rinky-dink
barbershop in Boston's South End,

my head shorn clean by a toothless
man who smelled of cherry tobacco

and Barbasol, who nattered on
about how *it just doesn't look right*

on a girl. Later, for my parents,
I'd say this was a practical act,

an evasion of catcalls and the wind
that whipped my hair into a knotted net

while I walked to class—not quite a lie,
but the more clandestine truth was Sue,

my freshman roommate, who wore a purple
tux to class, made friends on the subway,

introduced me most mornings to the guy
she'd picked up the night before, his name

always sweet and strange—Flower, perhaps,
or Moo. She kept bottles of fungi

in the mini-fridge and during finals
took Ecstasy with her friend, Goat, then slept

for three days while I wrote her paper
on mysticism. Sue shaved her head

over winter break and returned, stubble
abuzz with blond and blue streaks, gleaming

as if she'd been consecrated,
a Byzantine Madonna, her nimbus

bright, a jug of vodka cradled
like an infant, and when she hugged me,

I rubbed her smooth crown like the belly
of some golden statue, that touch a prayer.

Out on My Birthday, October 8, 1998

Ali is the first to reach the door, one hand
flashing her ID, the other rubbing a rogue streak of kohl
from beneath her eye. Her hair is tousled, still alive

with road-wind, a flutter of glitter raining
down from her shoulders. Em slices through the sweat
and perfume, leans her torso into the bar like it's a lover,

waits to be served. Ali has found a boy who looks like
Marilyn Monroe, all coifed blond curls and a stud like a birthmark
through his upper lip. Em and I watch them, a chaos

of gender gyrating in the sequined dark. Behind the bar,
the closed caption of the TV unravels the nightly news,
the young man tied to a fence in Wyoming.

His small face glows into the dim of the club,
casts Em's face in the slate hue that broadcasts
into the unlit room. Em turns away, picks at the red veins

of her lace shirt. The bartender reaches for a switch
and the night is suddenly silent and bright, all eyes
turned ungratefully toward the increasing volume

of the television. Somewhere behind me, in the crowd,
bursts a wrack of sobs, and a chorus of coughs trudges
uncomfortably around the room. The newscaster

has moved on, early snowstorm in Chicago.
The bartender hits the lights and the music whirrs
unsteadily back on. We are motionless, alone,

the hundreds of us, barely contained
within the plaster walls, the thin sheets
a barrier between us and the world.

When the Palm Reader Sees That You Have Two Life Lines, He Says You Must Choose One

I

Like the road
more traveled by,
your future has a use.
You will be tamped down,
firm as footsteps,
stretches of you littered
with loose change and leaves.
You will be paved with prints
not yours, marked by
what you have carried,
the dry dust of you
kicked up every time.
Subtle, silent,
faithful, you will be worn
with habit, or else
abandoned, weeds
growing through
your body, the cracked
surface of you. But
underneath,
the touch of roots,
worm-hollows, complex
vessels of under-skin.
Like the road
more traveled by,
no one will write poems
about you.

II

The road ahead
is not a road at all,
but a river, silt-strewn
rock-rub of your belly.
No birth but a fall
from the sky, you pool,
pouring over, sliding out.
You swallow fish whole,
spilling them in your wake,
ridges of sun strung out
on you. Electric, your current
floods every time
it rains, your body
rising up like a threat,
like a glorious wet
hunger. You freeze,
you thaw, you fuck
the dead things buried
inside you. You trickle
sickly in your dry spells.
You carry filth
the same as you carry
bronzed bodies.
In the end, you disappear,
absorbed, atomized, diffused
into one great body
more turbulent than you.

Coda, Codex, Codon

Take, for instance, the mayfly: the larva
    glutting itself on scum and detritus: a tactic
        culled through eons of relentless emerging
            and dying: that nonstop ingestion only just
                able to sustain a species. Each molting adult
            that flits above the stream like a luminaria
        guttering in the wind has its own pragmatic
    tradition to uphold: a sort of genetic anorexia:
gutless, it lives only to mate, to carry the magic
    to another generation. Always the same: DNA
        abandons all our intricacies to its own serpent
            growth, its self-love letting loose in operatic
                concerts of codons that call out: their song
            a metronomic tick run rampant: the thinnest
        gnomon under the sun slicing bits of electric
    time from the dial of the living. And yet, a coda:
cold moment when one of us lifts from the quag
    and seeks out another body: perhaps for comfort
        among the swarm: how the soft, deliquescent
            contours of the self lose shape, begin to hang,
                twisting into more exuberant form: a fantasia:
            gargoyle, cockatrice, some glowing benthic
        animal. How we collapse beneath the weight,
    the twining colubrine text that reads: chimera,
aberrance, survival of the mutant most fit.

Fiancée of Death

Because You're No Magician

I'm surprised when you offer
to cut me in two—
no glittered assistant
would trust you
with a saw. I mean the way you touch me
before you leave,
unfurling your fingers, a length of scarves
falling from your sleeve
onto the drinkable part of my throat—
or how you speak
in your sleep in words secret as Latin, the hocus pocus
mystique
of your somniloquy leaking into the dark.
I want my doves
tucked away in their compartment, safe
from the tug of your gloves
and the tip of your hat, the legerdemain
that lets you vanish
at will, shedding your trail of open-mouthed awe
and licorice
smoke, and reappear when your audience
thinks you've gone
for good, tossing off your cape
and waving your wand.

Love Song with Corset

When you say you cannot live without me, don't ask me why
I imagine you as a Devonshire patient—two ribs missing,
your lungs so vulnerable with only your thin skin left
to rebuff the world's advances—and me, a stay:
once what you put on and off for fashion,
now necessity: a busk, slab of oak
holding you up, erect, tightlaced.
I imagine you beneath me, metal
maiden to whom I molded myself,
or else real flesh: how I've rearranged all
your messy organs, how they grumble and thump
in your sleep. Tell me again how I touch you, all hooks
and ribbons, all ornament and constraint: tell me how it feels
to unthread me, to watch yourself taking form, flooding from me
like the rush of water through a baleen.

Elegy for the Night We Met

Nothing of astrological significance, no lunar eclipse,
and yet the night telescoped out: peeled labels
resting on the bar, the twinned imprint of your hips
on the stool, water-rings pooled on the tables

when we got up to dance, your arms that snaked
around me like an ampersand, and then, the walk
outside, the showering hiss of snow as it flaked
from branches, how it spread out like chalk

dust on the slate of the pavement. Some choice
I had, after all that, not to wish myself single,
not to wonder what it might be like to close

that night with more than a taste of your voice
like rusty water in my mouth, the quick tingle
of it on my lips, glints of ice where it froze.

Ballad for My Sweetheart the Drunk

By the end it became routine,
twelve hours of work followed
by six hours you called *second shift*,
the bar where we'd unload

and repack the day, you watching
me watching you caress
each bottle with your thumb, its small
twitch maybe meant to bless

that green glass, to daub its face with
the slightest of crosses.
Sometimes, the bartender, Kevin,
would threaten to toss us

out, mostly on those nights when you
cried for no reason—howled,
really—and I'd have to finesse
the jukebox 'til it growled

to life, Jeff Buckley wailing his
aching falsetto scream.
You'd sing along, *Hallelujah*,
as if this could redeem

all the nights we couldn't remember
stumbling home, how we must
have looked to passersby, our hands
lighting and rising just

over one another's shoulders,
as if we didn't know
which of us held the other,
which one would choose to go.

Epithalamium with Peeping Tom

What's this ring? Not the gold
hinge where the finger turns
away from the hand, floodgate for the *vena*

amoris, its sluicy
descent from the heart. No,
this ring: hole in the door, my eye a witness

to this mating practice,
all this finery: you,
the eager bird parading around the lek,

your alençon feathers
gathered in tufts, in white
pools around you. And him: his shaggy strut, jut

of his chin. How he glares
at the twin menisci
of your breasts, as though he would bore into them,

his vision an auger,
undoing your body
like a bomb. And who am I, lurking outside,

but a pin-up painted
on the flank of a plane,
a fiancée of death grinning through the gore,

and all around, this dark
frame: a reverse halo,
light winking out at the sight of all this love.

Mission Hill Lament

—after William Carlos Williams

Concrete is my own yard
where children learn
to play as they have always played,
but here they tumble and push
harder, to see whose bones
will be the first to break.
The first to break
was not my will, but my marriage.
The concrete is in bloom today
with webs of letters.
The letters I sent
weighed down my husband's mailbox,
threatened to burst its lock
with unanswered pleas
and unpaid bills.
He never had enough
to make replies worthwhile,
and today I was given notice—
two weeks before we are turned away.
Today my son told me
he does not need school—
out the classroom window,
on the other side of the fence, he saw
boys his age, smoking Newports,
their spray cans shooting letters.
I think that I would like
to go there,
breathe the last fumes of those letters,
and break my head on their concrete.

Broken Sonnet

Her car broke down at two in the morning,
its radiator pissing coolant
on the asphalt, the engine belching smoke
into the wind that shoved its icy hand
under her shirt. She stood in the shoulder,
without a phone or money for a ride home,
and thought of the tune-up she should have gotten
and the mechanic whose eyes kept running
up her thighs. Alone on the highway except
for nostrils of passing cars that flared
down the road and wouldn't stop in the night
for a stranger—she screamed at them until
a trucker stopped, and her life reduced to
what she tried to read in that man's eyes.

Elegy for Mrs. Donnell

What I remember most
is not her Scottish brogue,
the tough gust of her tongue,
but the way she dragged me
down the hallway, how heat
ran crimson from my pinched
right ear into my cheeks.
Her thick missile fingers
clamped on me while smoke froze
to my lips, while quick-eyed
girls thrust their hands under
faucets, swallowed their proof
down a mouth of dark drain.

What I remember, too,
are her eyes, silver snares,
the sinister *click clack*
snick of dentures. She said
I'd amount to less than
my mother had, less than
my sister, too. She said
that fifth-graders who cut
became teens who dropped out.
How was I to know then,
when I wished her dead, that
her husband was slowly
carrying out the job,
that soon he'd take a brick
to her head, how was I
to know what she knew
about being caught?

The Second Song of Miriam

> When the cloud went away from over the tent,
> Miriam had become leprous, as white as snow.
> —*Numbers 12:10*

He likes to make me
feel dumb. He doesn't trust me,
gives me half-concealed love.
I asked him to speak to me,
face to face, like a man.
His anger, kindled,
opened my skin, turned me
on the red spit of shame.

He visited me
with apologies, shade
and water in the wilderness.
My hands twitched
when he touched me.
He said he suffered, too,
so tired of trying
to keep me in place.

I used to sing
his praises to my family,
how he made me
want to dance at the edge
of the sea, shake my tambourine.
My wandering led me
to him, honeyed water
dried to salt on my ankles.

Clicks and Whirrs

Esprit d'Escalier

You want to appear aloof
after his comment, but *vendetta*
is branded like neon in the thick loam
of your skull, its buzz drowning the rustle
of his words just enough to hold back hysteria.
Whatever revenge you secret deep in the catacomb
of your mind is no use now, your bon mot like an orange
stripped of its rind, leaving you sweet. You grub, a sandpiper
worrying the same soggy spot over and again, that mealtime hustle
coming up with nothing, until finally the hunt for some venomous spoof
on his views turns up too late the tube from brain to mouth, its widening flange
pouring out your comeback, complex as the scaled geometries on the skin of a viper,
that showy design ornamenting your lips, dangling like so many violet racemes of wisteria,
its birth laborious as a monk's ministrations over a rare text, the illumination of one perfect letter.

Upon Learning that Sony Was Granted a Patent for Beaming Sensory Information Directly into the Brain

It was bad enough that night Ben, his mind
knotted with two hits of LSD, stunned
me with his sudden decision to slug
the shit out of my bathroom wall, his rough

treatment prompted by a newfound belief
that the devil, forever on the prowl
for another petty sinner or liege
minion, called from just beyond the rotund

lip of the tub, working his hoodoo jowl
away to get Ben's attention. No scuff
or crack showed afterwards to mark Ben's siege

on the tile and grout, just my empty shrug
when Ben asked where *he* went, my small relief
that the hospital wasn't hard to find.

To Mirah: In Utero: On Being Named

I lost control of my car one summer, blacked out
on the way to work: when I woke, I'd lost
a random taxonomy: *paper, sieve, sand dollar*:
stuck in some synapse between mind and tongue:
others lost in their fumble of letters: I found
driftwood on the river and called it *derby*:
my doctor gave me a name: *aphasia*: like Adam
knowing he'd gotten it right when he found
gecko or *ant lion* under a dead leaf: no doubt
there's a purgatory for lost language: the dark
burning-off before ascension: a lexicon
shaken loose from etymology: uprooted
rhizomes shucking their dirt: and you: swathed
in the hum of your name: all the world your alias.

Dysmorphia

After the stroke, I don't notice at first how one eyelid
    limps slightly lower than the other, or that the right
corner of my mouth turns down, even when I smile,
    as though gravity has stitched itself into one side
of my face and my remaining flesh, still weightless,

    hasn't caught on—I don't notice all this until, years
later, I try to cut my own hair, and there, with an old
    grow light trained like starshine on the nape of my neck,
I see it, caught in the angles between the two mirrors
    I'm using to make sure a fringe of hair falls evenly

across my cheek, and as I'm realizing that no manner
    of snipping will tip the scale of my face back into balance,
I spot the spider I chauffeured out the door earlier today,
    or one of her sisters, maybe, working her way back
in through the window beside the sink, and I wonder

    if she, too, is sentient enough to privilege the peach down
on her legs over the blue speckles of her back, if she
    has ever spun a web so lopsided that she welcomes the hand
that tears it from the wall, and then, the floor begins
    to whisper of its stains, the nubs of grout never properly

sanded down, the bathroom door lets out a groan
    for the wounded space between its edge and the jamb,
the carpet sucks its ugly tongue at its pills and frays,
    and outside, even outside, the trees are throwing themselves
against the wind, shaking their brown leaves to the ground.

The Amputation of My Brother's Finger

proves that some body parts are worth more
than others: at birth, his left index
finger, clinging like a remora
to his thumb: the thin slip of tissue
binding the two slit open, severed
to save that opposable digit.
What remains besides is the knuckle:
its crayon pink hump gleaming amidst
his ochre skin: that anomalous
smoothness somehow wondrous: the tonsure
of a monk: the silk inside one's cheek.
As for legacy: he recalls once
receiving detention for pointing
with his middle finger: and later,
restringing a bass: his right hand free
to work the frets. Still, he's never felt
phantom pain: no memory of sense
flickers in his cells: and when he tries
to imagine his hand whole, he says
it's never quite right: the forefinger
always more luminous or supple
than the others: its surface waxy
as an ex-voto hanging limply
on the wall of some sanctuary:
as if it was never his at all:
this body made to be offered up.

For My Brother, Who Cannot Cry

Holding you down, my knees like needles,
their bone-sharp weight against your spindly arms,
I pried open your eyelids, watching them part
like lips that want to hold in their world.

In this world, you never held still
long enough for me to put in the drops,
and sometimes you fought me so hard, the record
would skip on the turntable, its stuttering

drowned out by your wailing, the screams that forced
snot to bubble and bead on your upper lip.
I think of this now, the way you screamed,
not so much the sound but the great frightened gape,

the way your baby teeth shone
like hard milk against the pinkish dark,
the way your lips cracked and bled,
stretched to let out what you could not say.

The Weight

Inexplicable, the way the ham resting its haunches
in pineapple stew has prompted my father to resurrect

the weekend work of his youth, the days when to be a man
meant knowing how best to slaughter a pig.

Between forkfuls and careful napkin swipes, my father
pulls his mustache the way he does when he's nervous,

and it must be memory that makes him nervous now, as he softly
suggests that the challenge was the catch, the struggle to hold,

then one swift mallet stroke
with the weight of the body behind it.

Inexplicable, too, how his story conjures my own
youth, shot through with breakneck light,

the reckless speed of nights like the one
when, leaving late for some party, some date,

I backed his car into the mailbox
at the end of the drive. I never made it out

that night, though my father never said a word
as he hefted the mailbox like a monstrous hammer,

carried it inside, its head bumping against the burdened curve
of his shoulder, its door yawning like a tired child.

The Body Is No Machine

But it clicks and whirrs its history: for my father,
it begins at fifty-five: after cancer and remission,
the slink back through evolution: bird-wattle
descending from his throat: amphibian sheen
of his skin: lower lids pendant cocoons of silk:
and even inside, the valve of one ventricle
puckering like a fish, or my own lips: perched
at the beginning of a word, before I realize:
he's fallen asleep in his chair before the TV,
his body buoyant in its bath of noise and flicker:
and watching him, I too am growing old: ancient
as Lot's daughters: gazing at my father's naked
clockworks spinning in the darkness: tick of tooth
against tooth: steam and hiss of narrow escape.

Shift of Dirt

Genesis: On the Seventh Day

In the beginning, Eve slumbered
in the tall grasses, the blades stippling
her belly and cheek, bees lighting

to suck the sweet perspiration from her
shoulder. Painlessly inside her,
follicles ripened and blood ran

without reason. Eve dreamt of a world
in rows, fields of long fertile lines,
beasts yoked together, two by two.

Sunlight stained Eve's lids.
In the red veil of membrane
she watched breezes brush the trees,

saw fruit fall, its flesh split, its seeds
spill. Bodies filled the earth in her
dream, their breath tilling

the soil that stretched red
and wet with the river
that ran from her garden.

When You Ask Whether I Ever Played with Dolls

It's true—I loved my cousin's Barbies, how we dressed them
    in fig leaves we fashioned ourselves: violets

superglued to rubber bands. Usually, we'd tuck a pair together,
    snug in their makeshift bed, their arched feet

slipping against each other under the covers. No, the busty
    plastic femmes were never the problem:

what I couldn't abide were the stuffed infants, their puffy skin
    sewn from pantyhose, those eyes that winked

mercilessly open and shut with each shift in the center of gravity.
    Worst of all: my sister's Baby Alive, which ate

and shat Cheery Cherry sugar paste, its mindless automatism
    meant to imitate the digestive functions

of a bona fide baby, and perhaps that's what it did, the likeness
    a remarkable effect until its mysterious innards

were baffled by a blockage, a clump of sweetness lodged inside,
    and when my sister lifted Baby for her daily

ministrations, she found maggots spilling from its bowed lips.
    That night, my mother dumped all the dolls

in the pyre of our burn barrel, and though about this dramatic
    moment, my sister recalls only the smell—

melting plastic, scorched gingham—what haunts me is the sound,
    not just the hiss and pop of the flames,

but the hitching sobs of my sister as she wailed into the hollow between my mother's collarbone and shoulder.

Ballad for a Goth Chick

When Mary first saw Death, he had one arm
slung over her best friend's shoulder.
Mary could see how Susan had fallen
for someone like Death, the older

man, confident and debonair, who left
teenage Susan gasping for breath
the way none of her gangly classmates could.
She was captivated by Death,

and when he finally left her, Susan
never quite returned to normal.
Mary scarcely cared—she flirted with Death,
though he wasn't into formal

relationships. Death was sexy, he could
have any woman he wanted—
or man, for that matter—so Mary dressed
for Death. Her short black sheath flaunted

the legs she wrapped in tall boots and fishnets
that whispered and sighed as she walked.
She wanted Death to notice, willed his eyes
to follow her the way hers stalked

him. Sometimes Death filled Mary's thoughts, and when
she lay in bed, night dragging dark
skirts across the sky, she imagined him
shifting against her sheets, the arc

of his back pale as the moonlit surface
of the lake where she sometimes played
at suicide, wading in until her
head vanished. It was Death that made

her writhe up for air—after all, what if
Death came for her, what if today
Mary would lean into his kiss at last,
Death bending to meet her halfway?

Photograph of My Grandparents on the Farm, August 1945

They remember what the world was like

before it was split in two. As newlyweds,
they walked the rows of strawberry bushes,

the earth only red beneath their feet,

the sky only blue between the lace
of their fingers. Nothing hovered

on the horizon but the sun.

Sure, she worked in the factory, polishing
shell casings in the evenings, after her shift

at the paper. And he had seen his brother

run through the thresher, watched his mother
wilt in her bed. Death was a warm hand

pressed to the small of the back.

Then, the atom opened up, the magnificent
flower with its shredded corolla, its fiery

pistil, its thousand petals dusting

the land. They never saw the fevered burst
from their fields, but they remember the day

when Death became obsolete, his place filled

by the heat rushing from the crack of the world,
by a howl like the cry of Eve

being split from the side of man.

To the Ghost in My Front Yard

I'll assume you're there when the wind kicks up
the leaves in that patch that marks where you spun
your truck into the live oak: your scar: ground
where grass won't grow: I've filled it: filemot
piles slick with rain that glance the sodium
streetlight back: a humble sun: tapetum:
nocturnal eye opening in the earth:

this haunting isn't about seeing you:
it's how you see me: my hands first fumbling
then firm at your chest: my lips slick with blood
over yours: months after, the bits of glass
embedded in my knees begin to work
themselves out: splinters thin as hairs striking
at the air, glinting with their own faint light.

The Resurrectionist's Wife

He always returns—some nights
   from the pub, his skin radiant with smoke

   and the sweat of other men,
his breath hot as judgment against my ear—

or else from the graves, trailing
   the fecund dirt behind him—and then, too,

   the smell of other bodies
in our bed, the dull worm of it pressing

up to me when he does. Can
   this be the way he touches them, one hand

   on the abdomen, groping
in the dark for rotted spots? Does he trace

all the points where the scalpel
   will dig in, the bone-strapped organs huddled

   in the chest? Do their faces
bloom with blue flowers where the blood's gathered,

their cheeks dragging against his
   as he hauls them up—the loll of their head

   like an assent to desire
newly awake, its wink of furtive light?

Still Life

after anatomical illustrations from
The Fabric of the Human Body *(1543)*

When Vesalius posed his écorchés,
his skeletons, as living people—bone
and sinew brought to rest on a shovel's
handle, one leg kicked back against a wall
as though this corpse is stealing a moment
of refreshment, just a minute to breathe,
please, before he returns to the long dig—
when despite the detail, the striation
of muscle drawn thin as a lamella
on the page, the vegetation still creeps
and unfurls all around the flayed body,
it isn't so much the scene's oddity
that makes us cringe or laugh—it's the utter
congruity of our lives to the dead
man's, how we bare that same unnatural
grin for whoever's come to capture us,
how we pause, holding ourselves immobile
in the midst of the party, how silent
we are, each pull of air just audible
beneath the babble, subtle as the shift
of dirt under the weight of lifeless feet.

Sadie Imagines God

as a house with a hundred front doors, all
closed with locks she'll lick open, pick

with the grace of her tongue.

She'll sing her prayers, swing her hammer
of hallelujahs against oak and glass, send shivers

shimmying into cracks that spread

like legs or lips, thin rifts where she'll wedge
her eye like a dirty penny. She'll lie there, sprawled

out on the stoop, whistling

to herself, her feet hanging in the hydrangea,
one hand flicking over a hinge, the other

tracing figures in the dirt.

In Praise of the Myoclonic Jerk

After the tangle of my feet: here, wound
in the kick and hug of sheets: but elsewhere

urgent: I stumble, mid-gallop, midway
to touching a former love, her figure:

far-off: gleaming bright as a slick of egg:
or maybe my headlong rush is a flee

from her: that woman I betrayed: the light
she casts a fulmination, a brilliance

I try to escape. Whatever it is
I've conjured tonight: each firing synapse

blown by its own mysterious bellows:
it ends this way: impact: the fall before

safety or flesh is ever within reach:
electricity like a thrill of gold

through my body: pulse that calls me away
from desire, that speaks in its synchronous

voices: you are dying: you are waking.

photo by Leo Feng

Jennifer Perrine holds degrees in Religion, Art, English, and Creative Writing. Her work has appeared in various journals, including *Bellingham Review*, *Green Mountains Review*, *Nimrod*, *River Styx*, and *Southern Poetry Review*, among others. She lives in Des Moines, Iowa, and teaches writing, gender studies, and Holocaust studies at Drake University.

New Issues Poetry

Gerry LaFemina, *Window Facing Winter*

Steve Langan, *Freezing*

Lance Larsen, *Erasable Walls*

David Dodd Lee, *Abrupt Rural; Downsides of Fish Culture*

M.L. Liebler, *The Moon a Box*

Alexander Long, *Vigil*

Deanne Lundin, *The Ginseng Hunter's Notebook*

Barbara Maloutas, *In a Combination of Practices*

Joy Manesiotis, *They Sing to Her Bones*

Sarah Mangold, *Household Mechanics*

Gail Martin, *The Hourglass Heart*

David Marlatt, *A Hog Slaughtering Woman*

Louise Mathias, *Lark Apprentice*

Gretchen Mattox, *Buddha Box; Goodnight Architecture*

Lydia Melvin, *South of Here*

Carrie McGath, *Small Murders*

Paula McLain, *Less of Her; Stumble, Gorgeous*

Sarah Messer, *Bandit Letters*

Wayne Miller, *Only the Senses Sleep*

Malena Mörling, *Ocean Avenue*

Julie Moulds, *The Woman with a Cubed Head*

Marsha de la O, *Black Hope*

C. Mikal Oness, *Water Becomes Bone*

Bradley Paul, *The Obvious*

Jennifer Perrine, *The Body Is No Machine*

Katie Peterson, *This One Tree*

Elizabeth Powell, *The Republic of Self*

Margaret Rabb, *Granite Dives*

Rebecca Reynolds, *Daughter of the Hangnail; The Bovine Two-Step*

Martha Rhodes, *Perfect Disappearance*

Beth Roberts, *Brief Moral History in Blue*

John Rybicki, *Traveling at High Speeds* (expanded second edition)

Mary Ann Samyn, *Inside the Yellow Dress, Purr*